ACTIVITIES
SPORTS

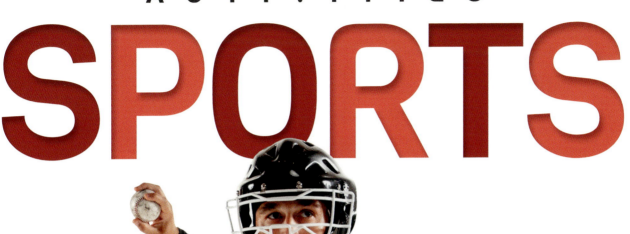

Written by
Kirsty Holmes

Genius Kid

American adaptation copyright © 2026 by North Star Editions, Mendota Heights, MN 55120. All rights reserved. No part of this book may be reproduced or utilized in any form or by any means without written permission from the publisher.

Sports © 2024 BookLife Publishing
This edition is published by arrangement with BookLife Publishing

sales@northstareditions.com | 888-417-0195

Library of Congress Control Number:
2024951996

ISBN
978-1-952455-22-3 (library bound)
978-1-952455-78-0 (paperback)
978-1-952455-61-2 (epub)
978-1-952455-42-1 (hosted ebook)

Printed in the United States of America
Mankato, MN
092025

Written by:
Kirsty Holmes

Edited by:
Elise Carraway

Designed by:
Ker Ker Lee

All facts, statistics, web addresses and URLs in this book were verified as valid and accurate at time of writing. No responsibility for any changes to external websites or references can be accepted by either the author or publisher.

Photo Credits – Images courtesy of Shutterstock.com, unless otherwise stated.

Cover – Ljupco Smokovski, MERCURY studio, Anton Vierietin, Andrey Burmakin, Ljupco Smokovski, Puttachat Kumkrong, Soho A Studio, Africa Studio, imagedb.com, Master1305. 2–3 – Anton Vierietin, Zamrznuti tonovi. 4–5 – Anton Vierietin. 6–7 – Master1305, Mega Pixel, Oleksandr Osipov. 8–9 – A.RICARDO, Marcos Castillo, YellowPaul, Master1305, Anton Vierietin. 10–11 – Tatiana Diuvbanova, Stefan Holm, Galina Barskaya. 12–13 – PeopleImages.com - Yuri A, Paolo Bona. 14–15 – Ljupco Smokovskil, wassiliy-architect, Artur Didyk, ComPix. 16–17 – kovop, Gilmanshin, sirtravelalot. 18–19 – Ljupco Smokovski, Roka Pics, Cristian Zamfir. 20–21 – artemisphoto, Master1305, GAS-photo, Design Projects. 22–23 – StockImageFactory.com, Anton Vierietin, jomphong.

CONTENTS

Page 4   Sports
Page 6   Key Words
Page 8   Solo Sports
Page 10   Partner Sports
Page 12   Team Sports
Page 14   Extreme Sports
Page 16   The Olympic Games
Page 18   Being a Good Sport
Page 20   Believe It or Not!
Page 22   Are You a Genius Kid?
Page 24   Glossary and Index

Words that look like this can be found in the glossary on page 24.

SPORTS

Sports are <u>physical</u> activities. They include an achievement or <u>competition</u>. Sports have set rules and <u>objectives</u>. Players compete against themselves or others to win.

Soccer

Ice hockey

Some sports are played alone. Others are played on a team.

Sports are more than a game, match, or meet. They involve both mental and physical skill. To be good at a sport, athletes practice the skills for that sport. They also work on their general fitness.

Basketball

KEY WORDS

Here are some key words about sports that every genius kid should learn.

ATHLETE
Someone who is skilled in a sport or physical activity.

RULES
Rules say what is and is not allowed to happen during sports. Rules help keep everyone safe. They make the competition fair.

OBJECTIVES

Objectives are what the competitors must do to win. For example, the objective of soccer is to score the most goals.

COMPETITION

In a competition, someone must win or an objective must be achieved. Runners might compete against their own best time. They may also race against others.

SOLO SPORTS

In solo sports, people compete on their own. The objectives of solo sports often focus on times or heights. They may also focus on distances or points.

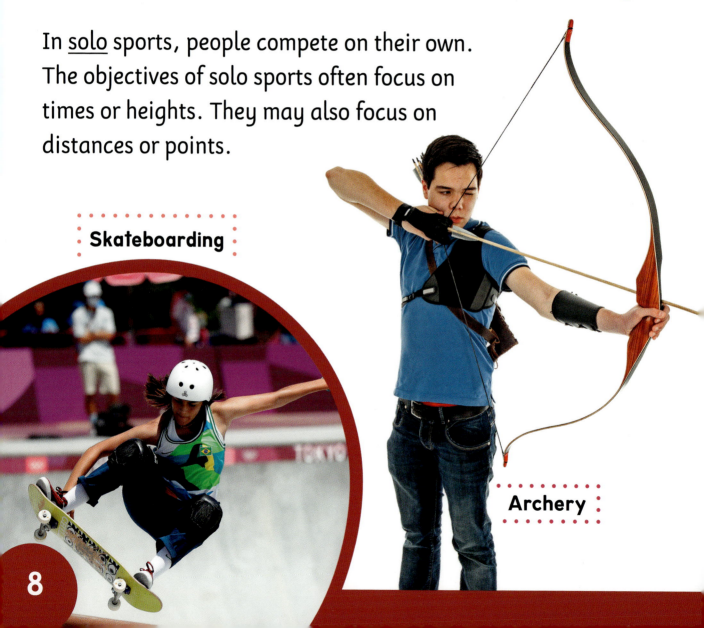

Skateboarding

Archery

Solo competitors try to beat their own best performances. Or they try to do better than others in a competition.

Swimming

Gymnastics

Track and Field

DID YOU KNOW?
There are many different types of gymnastics. Some types are tumbling, trampolining, and rhythmic gymnastics.

9

PARTNER SPORTS

Partner sports need two people. In most partner sports, the objective is to do better than your opponent. Partner sports include many net games. Net games are sports where two opponents are separated by a net.

Badminton

Table tennis

In some partner sports, you work alongside another person. You get scored together as a pair. You must work together to win. This is also called doubles, duos, or pairs.

Tennis doubles

TEAM SPORTS

Team sports have two or more groups of people playing against each other. Players on a team work together to win. The objective is to do better than the other team. Team sports are often scored with points.

Coach

DID YOU KNOW?
Coaches help players improve their play. They also help the team come up with a plan to win.

Team sports include:

- Soccer
- Rugby
- Football
- Basketball

- Baseball
- Lacrosse
- Ice hockey
- Volleyball

Can you think of any more?

....

On a sports team, everyone has a different job.

EXTREME SPORTS

Extreme sports are huge <u>feats</u> of speed, distance, height, strength, or <u>endurance</u>. In extreme sports, athletes push themselves to the limit.

Snowboarding

BMX, or Bicycle Motocross

Extreme sports are very exciting. They are also very risky. They should only be done by experienced and trained athletes.

Freestyle skiing

Kayaking

THE OLYMPIC GAMES

Every four years, thousands of athletes from more 200 countries come together to compete. They see who can win at different sports. These events are called the Olympic Games.

The Olympic rings represent the games.

First place wins a gold medal, second place wins silver, and third wins bronze.

The Paralympic Games show off the abilities of athletes with <u>disabilities</u>.

The first Olympic Games took place in ancient Greece.

DID YOU KNOW?
There are both Winter Olympics and Summer Olympics.

17

BEING A GOOD SPORT

Sports are also about being a good sportsperson. Being a good sport is about:

ALWAYS PLAYING FAIR
Win because you are great. Don't win by cheating.

BEING A TEAM PLAYER

Play, win, and lose as a team. You are all in it together. Respect your teammates and your opponents.

BEING A GOOD LOSER... AND A GOOD WINNER

Someone has to lose. Sometimes, it will be you. That is OK. Always congratulate your opponents.

BELIEVE IT OR NOT!

The International Olympic Committee says that some board games, including chess, count as sports.

Soccer is the world's most popular sport. It has more than three and a half billion fans worldwide.

Running, wrestling, and archery are some of the world's oldest sports.

Sports have even been played on the moon! Astronauts played javelin and golf there.

ARE YOU A GENIUS KID?

Now you are a genius kid in sports! Are you ready to win over your friends and family with a gold-medal quiz performance? On your marks, get set … GO!

Check back through the book if you are not sure.

1. The _____ Games is a big sporting competition held every four years.
2. What is the most popular sport in the world?
3. What are the medal colors for first, second, and third place?

Answers:
1. Olympic, 2. Soccer, 3. Gold (1st), silver (2nd), and bronze (3rd)

GLOSSARY

competition an event in which people go against each other to get or win something

disabilities physical or mental conditions that affect how people think, move, or interact with the world

endurance the ability to keep going even when things get difficult

feats amazing achievements that show courage, strength, or skill

objectives goals or purposes that people work to achieve

opponent someone you are competing against

physical to do with the body

solo done by one person alone, without help

INDEX

disabilities 17
games 5, 10, 16–17, 20, 23
moon 21
objectives 4, 7–8, 10, 12
Olympic Games 16–17

opponents 10, 19
pairs 11
rules 4, 6
teams 5, 12–13, 19
training 15